21-Day Devotional Journal

Today is a new day! What will you do with it?

Corinda Wilson

*Today, there is a new purpose, new opportunity, and
new chance waiting for you!
Will you accept the newness of today?
Whatever bothered you yesterday...
Whatever hurt you yesterday...
Whatever disappointed you yesterday...
Let it go!*

Walk in the "new" blessing of this day!

Table of Contents

DAY 1

Life's Lemons

Do you know the saying, "When life gives you lemons, make lemonade"? That is cute, but what if you are out of sugar? What if you do not have a vehicle that can get you to the store to get the sugar to make those sour lemons sweet?

Sometimes, our attitude is negatively impacted by the sourness and bitterness of life's situations. We forget how to use what we have on hand as a substitute until we can get exactly what we want or need. I encourage you to check your cabinets for some honey, stevia, or anything else you can use until you can get that sugar—that sweet spot of relief. In other words, find some joy amid the hard times in life.

Joy is a feeling of great pleasure and happiness. I believe "joy" is something you can find within yourself. The older saints sometimes say, "When I think of the goodness of Jesus and all He has done for me, my soul cries out, 'Hallelujah!'" or "God, if You never do anything else for me, You have already done enough." That is joy! Joy looks beyond current circumstances and finds pleasure and happiness in the feelings of gratefulness.

Let us open our personal cabinets and gratitude and use the sweetness of gratefulness to turn life's lemons into lemonade.

What is sour in your life right now that could use some sweetener?

If you are reading this, it is a new day! What will you do with it?

Based on today's reading, what is God speaking to you?

____

____

____

____

____

____

____

____

____

____

____

____

____

____

Today's Scripture:
1 Thessalonians 5:18 (ESV)
*"Give thanks in all circumstances;
for this is the will of God in Christ Jesus for you."*

Today, there is a new purpose, new opportunity, and new chance for you! Will you accept the newness of today? Whatever bothered you yesterday…whatever hurt you yesterday…whatever disappointed you yesterday…let it go! Walk in the "new" blessing of this day!

DAY 1

The Struggle is Real

My past (and sometimes present) struggle with anxiety and depression is real. I used to feel ashamed and embarrassed that I—a praying, praise and worshipping, Bible-reading "church girl"—could struggle with those feelings. The truth is, we all struggle with something, and the enemy knows exactly what it is. He studies us well by taking note of our weaknesses, insecurities, fears, and doubts. Then, he attempts to use those things against us to keep us bound and isolated in our pain, trying to prevent us from seeking God in our times of trouble.

Amid our struggles, our focus can shift and allow other distractions to settle in if we are not aware. At that point, the enemy comes in for the steal. He tries to take control by planting seeds of fear and doubt. His whispers will try to confuse and convince you of his lies, such as, "God does not love you," "God is not with you," or "God does not care about what you are going through."

Ephesians 6:11-18 instructs us to put on the full armor of God so that we can stand against the tricks of the enemy. There is power in knowing God and His Word. Now, that does not mean we will not have struggles in this life. However, it does mean that when they come, we already have what we need to defeat the enemy's advances. What we put in will come out when the enemy is in high pursuit, and the pressure in life is turned up. If we are not praying, studying the Word of God, and strengthening our foundation in Him daily, when the enemy attacks, we are left powerless.

Go pray. Go read. Go WIN! The victory is yours!

If you are reading this, it is a new day! What will you do with it?

Based on today's reading, what is God speaking to you?

Today's Scripture
1 Peter 5:8 (ESV)
*"Be sober-minded; be watchful. Your adversary, the devil, prowls around
like a roaring lion, seeking someone to devour."*

Today, there is a new purpose, new opportunity, and new chance for
you! Will you accept the newness of today? Whatever bothered you
yesterday…whatever hurt you yesterday…whatever disappointed you
yesterday…let it go! Walk in the "new" blessing of this day!

DAY 1

How Do You Pray?

I used to feel unsure about whether God heard my prayers. I wondered, "Am I doing this correctly? Are my prayers even reaching God's ears?" When those thoughts crossed my mind, I would try to adjust the way I prayed. I would find a quiet place, get on my knees, fold my hands, and close my eyes. I also incorporated scripture into my prayers. While those methods were not 'wrong,' my motivation was. One day, I received a message from the Lord that basically said, "Cut it out!" He told me I could come to Him in prayer just as I am and comfortably talk to him. It was then I breathed a sigh of relief. I realized changes in prayer come with building a relationship with Him and growth.

There are times when we are so focused on what we are "supposed to do" as Christians, we forget God knows us to our core. He knew us before we were in our mother's womb (Jeremiah 1:5). It is always better to be real with Him than "religious" in our interactions. God knows our hearts, and He desires a relationship with us.

Think about it like this: Can you truly have a real relationship with someone you cannot speak to comfortably?

My prayer for you today is that you go before God with authenticity. Your pretentious prayers do not impress Him. I pray He helps you to understand that He already knows what you need before you ask.

Praying is the personal connection that allows our relationship to grow deeper with the Lord.

If you are reading this, it is a new day! What will you do with it?

Based on today's reading, what is God speaking to you?

____

____

____

____

____

____

____

____

____

____

____

____

____

____

Today's Scripture
1 John 5:14-15 (KJV)
"And this is the confidence that we have in Him, that if we ask anything according to His will, He heareth us: and if we know that He hears us, whatsoever we ask, we know that we have the petitions that we desired of Him."

Today, there is a new purpose, new opportunity, and new chance for you! Will you accept the newness of today? Whatever bothered you yesterday…whatever hurt you yesterday…whatever disappointed you yesterday…let it go! Walk in the "new" blessing of this day!

DAY 1

Do Not Forget

Have you ever heard a testimony that moved you and strengthened your faith in God? At that moment, you felt peace, hope, and joy. Then, you moved on with your day. Time went by, and life happened. Along the way, you lost your faith, trust, and hope.

Let me encourage you not to forget. Remember the testimonies. If you need to, write them down so that you DO NOT FORGET.

Recently, a friend of mine shared a testimony during Bible Study concerning his trust in the Lord. He shared how his son had an asthma attack and how scary it was to watch him gasp for air, struggling to breathe. He rushed to the emergency room and, soon after, his son ended up in the ICU. My friend's father (who lived in a different state) was battling stage-4 cancer. While in the ICU with his son, he received a call saying his father's condition had taken a turn for the worse and that there was nothing else they could do for him. In response, he said he dropped his head and began to weep. There was absolutely nothing more he could do at that moment but put his trust in God as his son fought for his life, and his dad was losing his. A week later, his son recovered and was released from the hospital. My friend and his family could finally go to his father's bedside. Shortly after his arrival, his dad passed away.

While going through his trials, my friend was asked multiple times, "How is your faith?" He answered with, "Assuredly unshaken." He understood that God is sovereign, no matter the situation or circumstance.

When we place our trust in ourselves or our situations, we will fail every time. When we put our trust in God, He will never fail us. Proverbs 3:5-6 tells us to trust in the Lord with all our hearts and lean not to our own understanding. Will it be hard to trust in the Lord sometimes? Absolutely. It seems almost instinctual for us to lean to our own understanding. However, we must understand that we do not have the mental capacity to comprehend God's thoughts nor His ways (Isaiah 55:8).

When you feel weak or as if your faith is taking a hit, pull out those testimonies and read them. Always remember God is still able, and He still performs miracles.

DO NOT FORGET!

If you are reading this, it is a new day! What will you do with it?

Based on today's reading, what is God speaking to you?

____

____

____

____

____

____

____

____

____

____

____

____

____

____

Today's Scripture
Proverbs 3:5-6 (ESV)
"Trust in the Lord with all your heart, and do not lean on your own understanding. In all your ways, acknowledge Him, and He will make straight your paths."

Today, there is a new purpose, new opportunity, and new chance for you! Will you accept the newness of today? Whatever bothered you yesterday…whatever hurt you yesterday…whatever disappointed you yesterday…let it go! Walk in the "new" blessing of this day!

DAY 1

The Step Stool

Have you ever wanted to be "the boss"? Many people do and are willing to do whatever it takes to be on top. I wonder how many people consider they may not be boss material. For some, their purpose may merely be the "step stool." Picture getting down on your hands and knees to give someone a boost (not literally, but figuratively). It may be a big pill for some to swallow, but instead of rising to the top, your GIFT may be to help someone else get there.

Time and time again, I have watched my husband serve as the step stool. Honestly, it enraged me at times (admittedly, I was not as humble as he). Through the years, though, God has used my husband to show me I must be willing to be a step stool in life.

Ultimately, when God has something just for us, nothing and no one can take it away. Simply put: Being the step stool will not hinder your blessing if God has it to give to you. Helping others will not prevent you from getting to where God wants you to be.

Before my revelation, I used to think my husband was ridiculous when he helped others because it seemed he was in a place of stagnancy. It appeared he was being used…being stepped on. All the while, God worked things out for his good as he continued serving those around him. My husband has had unimaginable favor, and thus, we (his family) have been shown favor as well. He has not had to elevate himself because God is taking care of that for him.

Focus on being selfless. Show the love of God through helping others, then watch how things work out for your good. It has been one of the greatest lessons I have learned along life's journey.

If you are reading this, it is a new day! What will you do with it?

Based on today's reading, what is God speaking to you?

Today's Scripture
Galatians 6:9 (KJV)
*"And let us not be weary in well-doing:
for in due season, we shall reap, if we faint not."*

Today, there is a new purpose, new opportunity, and new chance for you! Will you accept the newness of today? Whatever bothered you yesterday…whatever hurt you yesterday…whatever disappointed you yesterday…let it go! Walk in the "new" blessing of this day!

DAY 1

Asking

Do we ever stop and think about those things for which we ask God? It is easy to get caught up in asking for what we want in our prayer and intimate time with God, but how often do we ask Him for our wants in accordance with His will for our lives? John 15:7 begins with, "If you abide in Me…" and ends with, "…it will be done for you." When spending time in the Word and getting to know our Heavenly Father, the things we ask for would not be superficial. Our hearts and minds would be transformed, thus becoming Kingdom-minded and positioned to request what is in line with God's purpose-filled desires are for our lives. As our faith matures and we grow closer to Him, selfish prayers such as, "Lord, bless me with riches," should fade away.

In the Bible, King Solomon had a heart for God. One night, God appeared to him in a dream and asked what it was that he desired (1 Kings 3:5-14). Solomon could have asked for anything, but he chose wisdom—not the usual request for long life, wealth, or doom for his enemies I imagine God was used to receiving. It pleased God that Solomon asked for wisdom because that made him willing to be led by the Lord in a mighty way for the Kingdom of God. The icing on the cake was when God told Solomon he would receive wealth and glory if he continued to walk in God's ways and follow His commandments. How amazing is that?

As you "ask," I encourage you to spend time with God and, in your asking, reflect on what God has put you on this Earth to do to build His Kingdom and glorify His Name. "Ask" for things that will line up with His will for your life, and watch Him be pleased with you, blessing you abundantly.

If you are reading this, it is a new day! What will you do with it?

Based on today's reading, what is God speaking to you?

____

____

____

____

____

____

____

____

____

____

____

____

____

Today's Scripture
John 15:7 (ESV)
*"If you abide in me, and my words abide in you,
ask whatever you wish, and it will be done for you."*

Today, there is a new purpose, new opportunity, and new chance for you! Will you accept the newness of today? Whatever bothered you yesterday…whatever hurt you yesterday…whatever disappointed you yesterday…let it go! Walk in the "new" blessing of this day!

DAY 1

Comfortable Being Uncomfortable

I have known for years that God has gifted me to write—a gift that has been confirmed by others. Initially, I allowed fear to control what I knew I was anointed to do, causing me to start and then stop writing a few books. Time after time, I chose not to push through my fears, doubts, and insecurities. I made it about me when it was bigger than me.

Now, I often encourage myself by affirming; I am smart, purpose-filled, equipped, and chosen.

There may be times when we find ourselves fading into the background of life. With so many distractions in the world, the noise can become overwhelming and cause us to retreat. We might lose our motivation and wonder if we will ever walk in our God-given purpose or receive all that God has for us in this life. Just then, the discouraging whispers begin, preventing our attempts to move beyond stagnancy, and we start to look like how we feel: defeated. We are not meant to be stagnant; we choose to be. That may be a hard truth to accept, but we all have free will. Part of having free will is making choices.

Furthermore, we are not gifted for our own gain; we are gifted to bless others. When we truly begin to comprehend the magnitude of that responsibility in our purpose, we will not allow the discomfort of our fears, insecurities, and inadequacies to stop us. Fear is a distraction.

God has given you a purpose. Are you choosing to walk in that purpose each day? I challenge you to get comfortable with being uncomfortable. You are already gifted and equipped to walk in God's purpose for your life.

If you are reading this, it is a new day! What will you do with it?

Based on today's reading, what is God speaking to you?

Today's Scripture
Philippians 1:6 (ESV)
*"And I am sure of this, that He who began a good work in you
will bring it to completion at the day of Jesus Christ."*

Today, there is a new purpose, new opportunity, and new chance for you! Will you accept the newness of today? Whatever bothered you yesterday…whatever hurt you yesterday…whatever disappointed you yesterday…let it go! Walk in the "new" blessing of this day!

DAY 1

Ministering at Home

One day, while in conversation with my mother, she asked me, "Have you shared any of your struggles with your daughters? If so, did you use them as teaching points to minister to them, pour the Word of God into them, or show them how God helps believers through their issues?" Admittedly, I had never considered how my life story could be used as a teaching point for my girls.

The following day, I got up, spent time talking with God, and journaled. One of the things I asked God for was the opportunity to minister to someone—anyone—that day. I had no idea that "someone" would be my youngest daughter the very next hour.

While she was in the bathroom getting ready for school, we began talking about her recent bad dreams. That was my opening! I spoke to her about fear, tricks and tactics of the enemy, and how we can use God's Word as a powerful tool to defeat the devil. Finally, I spoke life to her spirit by sharing with her that she was "chosen" by God and explained she has a purpose on this Earth to do great things each day.

Our conversation blessed me. The sparkle in her eyes when I told her that the more of God's Word she places in her heart and mind, the more powerful she would be, was a beautiful reminder of the importance of my purpose as her mother.

While we are out ministering to the world, let us remember those in our home who look to use for guidance, especially the little ones.

If you are reading this, it is a new day! What will you do with it?

Based on today's reading, what is God speaking to you?

____

____

____

____

____

____

____

____

____

____

____

____

____

____

____

Today's Scripture
Proverbs 22:6 (KJV)
_"Train up a child in the way he should go:
and when he is old, he will not depart from it."_

Today, there is a new purpose, new opportunity, and new chance for you! Will you accept the newness of today? Whatever bothered you yesterday…whatever hurt you yesterday…whatever disappointed you yesterday…let it go! Walk in the "new" blessing of this day!

DAY 1

Progression, Not Perfection

rogression, not perfection—three words a dear brother-in-Christ, talented musician, and friend often said during choir rehearsal. He came into my life at a time when I felt immense pressure not to make many mistakes. I had taken over as our praise team's worship leader and was the structured, "it must be perfect" person. Before he came, it was just me leading one of the most essential ministries in any church: the music ministry. I had no idea what I was doing, but I was determined to do it well!

With him by my side, we worked together very well and became like family. In a short amount of time, I gained a "little brother." (You would laugh at the term "little brother" if you saw how big he is—big, but gentle and jolly.) When we first met, his lifestyle was one I was unfamiliar with; chilled, easy-going, and peaceful. I recall how irritated my spirit would be when he heard sour notes sung but still provided encouragement and opportunity for all. His favorite words would ring out, "Progression, not perfection." Internally, I would scream, "Are you SERIOUS?!"

As I reflect on the experience gained from that position, along with working with "little brother," I realize just how much I learned about life. Progression is the process towards achievement. Perfection is often an unattainable concept (outside of God) that can lead to constant disappointment.

If we are progressing in life—no matter what the journey looks like— we are at least trying, getting better, and moving forward. If we do not allow room for grace because it looks like perfection will not be attained by ourselves or others, we force ourselves to stay in a stagnant place.

If you are reading this, it is a new day! What will you do with it?

Based on today's reading, what is God speaking to you?

____

____

____

____

____

____

____

____

____

____

____

____

____

Today's Scripture
Philippians 3:12 (ESV)
*"Not that I have already obtained this or am already perfect,
but I press on to make it my own because Christ Jesus has made me His own."*

Today, there is a new purpose, new opportunity, and new chance for you! Will you accept the newness of today? Whatever bothered you yesterday…whatever hurt you yesterday…whatever disappointed you yesterday…let it go! Walk in the "new" blessing of this day!

DAY 1

Social Media

I often jokingly say, "Social media is of the devil." Although said in jest, there may be some merit to that statement—although social media is used for many great things and opportunities as well. Let us dig deeper…

How many times have you logged into your social media account and found yourself experiencing feelings of anger, jealousy, insecurity, discontentment, sadness, fear, or lust—just to name a few? If you are completely honest here, you may find you fell victim to what I call "Social Media Sin." If you are not careful, the wrong side of social media can consume you.

Lately, I have felt the need to do a social media self-check. How do I feel when I am scrolling? Is what I see life-giving or life-taking? Is it a platform I frequent out of habit or boredom? Is it a necessity? Does it cause me to sin?

Those questions are important, and I encourage you to ask yourself them as well. Often, the thing that feels small and insignificant (i.e., social media) can be the face of turmoil in your life. Somewhere along the way, you may have been shaped to believe that you may miss out on something if you do not indulge. What if that time spent scrolling was, instead, spent with God—time that you can pray or read His Word?

I frequently reference distractions because I know they are real. Do not sleep on the enemy. Know that his attempts to distract come in many forms, with social media being one of them. Daily, the choice is ours.

May we all choose wisely.

If you are reading this, it is a new day! What will you do with it?

Based on today's reading, what is God speaking to you?

____

____

____

____

____

____

____

____

____

____

____

____

____

Today's Scripture
Romans 12:2 (ESV)
"Do not be conformed to this world, but be transformed by the renewal of your mind, that by testing, you may discern what is the will of God, what is good and acceptable, and perfect."

Today, there is a new purpose, new opportunity, and new chance for you! Will you accept the newness of today? Whatever bothered you yesterday…whatever hurt you yesterday…whatever disappointed you yesterday…let it go! Walk in the "new" blessing of this day!

DAY 1

Turbulence

One thing I fear the most in life is flying. I have flown many times, and each time, I felt very unsettled. No matter how hard I tried to relax, pray, and allow the peace of God to comfort me throughout the flight, fear always kicked in.

A memorable moment in the skies for me happened on October 12, 2019. It was the worst, turbulent-laden flight I have ever experienced. I recall looking over at my girls to see how well they were handling it. I did not let them see just how shaken I was, though. As their mother, I understood my reaction would control their response. If I panicked, then they would have panicked, too. Therefore, I chose to show them peace and calm through the turbulence.

Thinking back on that day, I smile and consider how God works. Before boarding, I prayed for a smooth flight. Although that is not what I received, I was not disappointed or upset because God did not answer my prayer. Why? Because there was a valuable lesson in the turbulence.

There will be some situations and circumstances in life that we must endure. Life will not always feel good. As a matter of fact, it can be downright scary and feel unsettling at times—much like the turbulent flight I was on that day. However, after having "gone through," we will find our faith and trust in God have increased when we get to the other side.

How can we know God will do "it" for us if there is no "it" for us to endure? Take that question into consideration in all areas of your life. Know that someone else is watching how you go through the turbulence. What is it that you are showing them? Faith or fear?

If you are reading this, it is a new day! What will you do with it?

Based on today's reading, what is God speaking to you?

Today's Scripture
James 1:2-4 (ESV)

"Count it all joy, my brothers, when you meet trials of various kinds, for you know that the testing of your faith produces steadfastness. And let steadfastness have its full effect, that you may be perfect and complete, lacking in nothing."

Today, there is a new purpose, new opportunity, and new chance for you! Will you accept the newness of today? Whatever bothered you yesterday…whatever hurt you yesterday…whatever disappointed you yesterday…let it go! Walk in the "new" blessing of this day!

DAY 1

Success

In the past, when I thought about where I wanted to be at specific points in my life versus where I was, disappointment settled in. I looked to my left and right, noticing how it appeared my peers were thriving in what the world defined as "success." I began to compare myself to them, which caused a flood of negative thoughts to consume my mind. Before I knew it, I was in a dark place that was fraught with depression, self-pity, and self-doubt.

Has that ever happened to you?

As believers, we must realize "success" is relative. It may seem as if we are not successful according to the world's standards, but it is how God sees us that should matter the most. We must ask ourselves, "Is God pleased with what I have done with my time on this Earth up to this point in my life?"

Do not torture yourself with time. Instead, ask yourself, "Have I been intentional with the time I have been given? Who have I helped to understand who God is? Who have I led to salvation? Who have I been kind to, shown love to, and been gentle with?"

Lastly, I want to ask you this: Are you God's hands and feet on this Earth, or are you too busy looking to your left and right while chasing the world's definition of "success"?

Remember this: Comparison is the robber of joy!

If you are reading this, it is a new day! What will you do with it?

Based on today's reading, what is God speaking to you?

____

____

____

____

____

____

____

____

____

____

____

____

____

____

Today's Scripture
Galatians 1:10 (ESV)

"For am I now seeking the approval of man, or of God? Or am I trying to please man? If I were still trying to please man, I would not be a servant of Christ."

Today, there is a new purpose, new opportunity, and new chance for you! Will you accept the newness of today? Whatever bothered you yesterday…whatever hurt you yesterday…whatever disappointed you yesterday…let it go! Walk in the "new" blessing of this day!

DAY 1

God is Real

During a recent Bible study my daughters and I had, we explored the Old Testament Book of Leviticus, where it spoke of the laws the Jewish people were required to follow as a nation. We discussed the sacrifices the people had to make as an atonement for their sins, along with the fact that those practices are no longer necessary because Christ came and died for our sins as the ultimate sacrifice. I then began to sense my girls had some questions in their spirits that needed definitive answers.

I am aware that children might have difficulty processing the validity of some biblical information. Some adults often struggle with the same. For many of us, we need a sign—a miracle—that proves God is REAL.

As our study continued, my wheels began to turn, but all I could offer my children at that moment was the grace to ask their questions. I explained they must get to know God and read the Bible for themselves, no matter what they were told. I also warned that having all the answers will never happen because that is where faith comes into action.

Then, it happened. I was reminded of a time when I knew God was, indeed, real. I shared that story with them, and I will share it now with you…

When my youngest daughter was around two years old, she woke up one morning crying inconsolably. I ran to her room and found a beautiful but distraught wet-faced little girl. My first thought was that she was physically hurt, but that was far from the case. I picked her up, held her in my arms, and asked her, "What's wrong?"

Her answer blew me away. She looked up at me, still crying uncontrollably, and said, "I miss Him."

I was confused. "Who do you miss?" I asked.

"I miss God. I want to go back to be with Him."

"You miss GOD?" I asked, the surprise evident in my voice.

Still inconsolable, her response was simply, "I want to go back."

I will never forget that life-changing morning. If I had any doubts, that was a sure sign to me that God IS real. My daughter had a few more "God" moments as a young child, but those memories slowly disappeared as she grew older. Today, she has no recollection of those moments, but I do…and I always will.

We may never get the answers to all our hard questions concerning God, but I pray He shows you that He IS real.

If you are reading this, it is a new day! What will you do with it?

Based on today's reading, what is God speaking to you?

____

____

____

____

____

____

____

____

____

____

____

____

____

____

Today's Scripture
Hebrews 11:1 (KJV)
"Now, faith is the substance of things hoped for,
the evidence of things not seen."

Today, there is a new purpose, new opportunity, and new chance for you! Will you accept the newness of today? Whatever bothered you yesterday…whatever hurt you yesterday…whatever disappointed you yesterday…let it go! Walk in the "new" blessing of this day!

DAY 1

It's Gonna Be BIG!

In the song "BIG" by Pastor Mike, Jr., the lyrics of the chorus are:

"God's gonna open the windows of Heaven, pour me out a blessing; won't have room to contain it, won't even try to explain it, 'cause it's gonna be BIG!"

That song is often on 'repeat' in my mind. It gives me hope when I cannot see what God has planned for me or when I do not yet see anything happening.

Have you ever been in that place where it seemed you were not progressing? You might have been working towards something and became disheartened because it was not working out the way you envisioned. As a result, you might have felt unmotivated because every time you took a step forward, fear and doubt found their way to the front of the line. The next thing you knew, you were battling with not knowing which direction to go, but you did not give up. You persevered! Look at you now!

God has a way of sending messages of hope when He knows we need it the most. He sends messages of perseverance and confidence in Him when we cannot seem to find them within ourselves. Sometimes, we have a dire need for messages of hope and a future, much like the people in exile needed in Jeremiah 29:11.

How about some encouragement for today?

Keep going! Do not give up! God has not forgotten about you! The same way you see Him blessing others, He will do the same for you. It's gonna be BIG! NOTHING is impossible with God (Luke 1:37)!

If you are reading this, it is a new day! What will you do with it?

Based on today's reading, what is God speaking to you?

____

____

____

____

____

____

____

____

____

____

____

____

____

____

Today's Scripture
Jeremiah 29:11 (KJV)
"For I know the thoughts that I think toward you,' saith the Lord, 'thoughts of peace, and not of evil, to give you an expected end.'"

Today, there is a new purpose, new opportunity, and new chance for you! Will you accept the newness of today? Whatever bothered you yesterday…whatever hurt you yesterday…whatever disappointed you yesterday…let it go! Walk in the "new" blessing of this day!

DAY 1

Help!

Three words that are hard to admit are, "I need help!" When we do not admit it, we often continue to suffer in silence. We smile when we want to cry, and slowly but surely, our mental health begins to deteriorate. Eventually, the truth will unmask what our pride was trying to hide: our state of brokenness.

"I need help!" Say it aloud! It is okay to cry out in our time of need. We all need support at various points in our lives. We all have trials and tribulations seasons that do not feel good, but they serve to perfect our faith.

"I need help!" Get help for whatever "it" is—your marriage, mental health, parenting, spiritual guidance, fitness, loneliness, etc. Get help now! You are not alone, and God has gifted others to assist you, no matter what you are facing.

The enemy uses isolation to destroy us. He makes us feel alone in our hardships and pain, which causes feelings of guilt and shame about our thoughts and feelings. The enemy takes great joy in overwhelming our thoughts. He chastises followers of Christ, making it unsafe to feel anything outside of gratitude, thankfulness, and joy.

We are beautifully human, made in God's image and likeness. God also knows what we are up against in this world. The victory is already ours, though. Do you choose to receive it today?

No matter what you are facing, there is HELP for you. Go and get it!

If you are reading this, it is a new day! What will you do with it?

Based on today's reading, what is God speaking to you?

____

____

____

____

____

____

____

____

____

____

____

____

____

____

____

Today's Scripture
Ephesians 6:12 (NIV)
"For our struggle is not against flesh and blood, but against the rulers, against the authorities, against the powers of this dark world, and against the spiritual forces of evil in the heavenly realms."

Today, there is a new purpose, new opportunity, and new chance for you! Will you accept the newness of today? Whatever bothered you yesterday…whatever hurt you yesterday…whatever disappointed you yesterday…let it go! Walk in the "new" blessing of this day!

DAY 1

Speak Life

Do you believe life and death lie in the power of the tongue? Do you believe your words have power?

There is a book by Charles Capps titled *The Tongue: A Creative Force.* That book challenged me to reflect on the words I speak. I began to think about the words I allowed to escape from my lips without much thought, as well as words that could bless or curse myself or others. To my dismay, I realized that many times, my tongue was weaponized. I have often spoken defeat, negativity, doubt, and despair over my own life without knowing that I was doing so. Time and again, I unknowingly gave the enemy power against me with my own words.

Think about that for a moment. Have you ever complained that something was "never" going to change or get better? Have you ever said something like, "I don't feel like my pain is ever going to go away" or "This is something I will just have to live with"? If so, you gave that problem a little more momentum in your life.

As believers, we must use the Word of God to speak life to our problems, not death. An example of that concept would be saying something like, "I may have some pain right now, but the Word says by His stripes, I am healed. I believe my healing is on the way."

The good news is that you can start speaking life to yourself today! I challenge you to change your words and observe the positive difference it makes.

If you are reading this, it is a new day! What will you do with it?

Based on today's reading, what is God speaking to you?

Today's Scripture
Proverbs 18:21 (KJV)
*"Death and life are in the power of the tongue:
and they that love it shall eat the fruit thereof."*

Today, there is a new purpose, new opportunity, and new chance for you! Will you accept the newness of today? Whatever bothered you yesterday…whatever hurt you yesterday…whatever disappointed you yesterday…let it go! Walk in the "new" blessing of this day!

DAY 1

Chasing Purpose

Are you driving yourself crazy trying to figure out what your God-given purpose is? You see others operating in their gifts and talents, living a meaningful life, yet you are still searching. Daily, you ask God, "What is my purpose?" and feel as if you are no closer to knowing than you were years ago. You might be frustrated and almost at the point of giving up. You may even tell yourself that where you are is where you will stay.

What if I told you that chasing purpose is a trap? The chase will cause you not to appreciate the opportunities of today. Each day holds a purpose, so why not use this day to live on purpose? God knows you and has prepared you with everything you need to be about His business today! Do not be tempted to make what is simple so complicated. Living life with purpose is no secret, as it is the same for us all! Are you ready to hear and live your purpose? Here it is: Fear God and follow His commandments.

You might be wondering, "How is that walking in my God-given purpose?" If you are focused on reverencing God each day and do what He instructed in His Word, He will guide your footsteps and direct your path daily.

There is a beautiful prayer in Matthew 6:9-13 (KJV). I share it with you below. I believe it will bless you as you begin to walk with purpose each day instead of chasing it.

"Our Father, which art in Heaven, Hallowed by Thy name. Thy kingdom come. Thy will be done in Earth, as it is in Heaven. Give us this day our daily bread. And forgive us our debts, as we forgive our debtors. And lead us not into temptation but deliver us from evil: for thine is the kingdom, and the power, and the glory, forever. Amen."

If you are reading this, it is a new day! What will you do with it?

Based on today's reading, what is God speaking to you?

____

____

____

____

____

____

____

____

____

____

____

____

____

____

Today's Scripture
Proverbs 19:21 (ESV)
*"Many are the plans in the mind of a man,
but it is the purpose of the Lord that will stand."*

Today, there is a new purpose, new opportunity, and new chance for you! Will you accept the newness of today? Whatever bothered you yesterday…whatever hurt you yesterday…whatever disappointed you yesterday…let it go! Walk in the "new" blessing of this day!

DAY 1

The Blessing in the Burden

There have been several times when I thought I would not make it another day. Anxiety had its stronghold on me, and I could not see my way out. Many times, I asked God, "Why can't I conquer this completely?" I have even pleaded with Him to remove the burdens while crying a sea of tears, year after year. At times, my heart was heavy, and I wondered if I would have to walk in the misery my whole life, carrying the cross of anxiety. I had learned to wrap it beautifully and mask it gracefully so that others could still see the God in me and not the burdens I bore.

I recall when God spoke to me through a devotional. He told me there was a blessing in my anxiety, in that it kept me close to Him. I was left speechless and had to sit and think about what He said. "Really, God? You mean to tell me that one of the ugliest things I battle—the thing that keeps me in cycles of what seems like pain and depression—is a blessing?" I questioned. Surely, that could not have been the case, right?

I began to think about the times in my 15-year battle when my anxiety was at its worst. They were all times when it was critical that I drew closer to God. Those were the times I prayed more, read more, sought understanding, and could hear the voice of the Lord clearly. That revelation blew my mind! I understood what God revealed, and today, I am stronger than ever!

No matter what you are dealing with, know that you do not walk alone. God is with you. Those times when you may feel weak, defeated, and as if you cannot go on, cry out, "BUT GOD!" Allow His wonder-working power to be made perfect in your weakness. Walk in the victory that is yours through Christ Jesus!

If you are reading this, it is a new day! What will you do with it?

Based on today's reading, what is God speaking to you?

____

____

____

____

____

____

____

____

____

____

____

____

____

Today's Scripture
2 Corinthians 12:9-10 (NIV)

"But He said to me, 'My grace is sufficient for you, for My power is made perfect in weakness.' Therefore, I will boast all the more gladly about my weaknesses, so that Christ's power may rest on me. That is why, for Christ's sake, I delight in weaknesses, in insults, in hardships, in persecutions, in difficulties. For when I am weak, then I am strong."

Today, there is a new purpose, new opportunity, and new chance for you! Will you accept the newness of today? Whatever bothered you yesterday…whatever hurt you yesterday…whatever disappointed you yesterday…let it go! Walk in the "new" blessing of this day!

DAY 1

God's Plans

I do not know about you, but I have spent a great deal of my life trying to make my own path and my own plans. Doing so has only led to feelings of unfulfillment and discontentment. I am a military spouse and homemaker. I did not want to accept those things as being exclusively who I am, so I constantly searched for more and more…and more.

I desired a career title so that I would feel accepted by society. Every time someone asked me the dreaded question, "What do you do??" I wanted to hide. My response felt so insignificant. Often, I was embarrassed by it. I frequently prayed for God to open doors for me and show me my purpose in life, only to be left feeling dejected when the answer was not what I wanted to hear. I believed I deserved to be important, make a lot of money, and have a title. After all, I earned a master's degree! "Doesn't that count for something?" I often asked myself.

God had to show me that my will for my life and His will for my life were not one and the same. I learned that no matter what I plan, God's purpose for creating me will always override what I believe it should be. As a close friend of mine says, "I am a square peg, trying to fit myself into a round hole." It will not work!

I can finally see that God has been making provisions for me to walk in His purpose all along. I am chosen! I am not meant to be what I wanted to be because I am called to greatness as a mighty woman of God! Staying at home allowed me the freedom to walk in my purpose, although for the longest time, I could not see that advantage.

What is it that you are seeking or holding onto? Does God keep closing doors that you keep trying to open? Is your "yes" trying to overpower His "no"?

I implore you to think long and hard about your purpose and path in life. If you know you are walking in your plan and living by your will, my prayer is that you surrender to God's plan. He desires that you have life more abundantly (John 10:10).

If you are reading this, it is a new day! What will you do with it?

Based on today's reading, what is God speaking to you?

____

____

____

____

____

____

____

____

____

____

____

____

____

Today's Scripture
John 10:10 (ESV)
*"The thief comes only to steal and kill and destroy.
I came that they may have life and have it abundantly."*

Today, there is a new purpose, new opportunity, and new chance for you! Will you accept the newness of today? Whatever bothered you yesterday…whatever hurt you yesterday…whatever disappointed you yesterday…let it go! Walk in the "new" blessing of this day!

DAY 1

Stay Focused

Years ago, a stockpile of incidents happened in my life in the span of a week. I got a cold, passed out, and was rushed to the emergency room. I could not see clearly or drive for weeks after that. I relocated to a new state, was in a car accident with my family (we were all okay), cared for a sick child who had to go to the emergency room, and more. Ouch! That was one of the toughest weeks thus far that my family and I have had to endure. I am thankful to God that even amid those issues, I remained mentally sound and could still focus.

It is not always easy to focus when life gets chaotic, and it feels like everything around us is literally falling apart at the seams. However, we need to understand that chaos can be deceptive. It is a trick the enemy can use to tempt us to have doubt, change course, or worse…give up!

At different times during that week full of transitions, I struggled with my emotions but did not miss a single day of my devotion time with God. By standing on His Word, I was able to withstand the poking and prodding of the enemy. The dialogue between the enemy and I went a little something like this:

Enemy: "You can't stand change, and this one is really too big for you to handle. You will never be happy here, far away from what is comfortable and familiar. You never wanted this unstable military life anyway! Now, look at you. You are moving again! You will never be settled—mentally nor physically."

Me: "How clever… You almost got me because you definitely know my weaknesses, BUT I read in Philippians 4:13 that I can do all things through Christ, who strengthens me. In Philippians 4:6-7, I am instructed to be anxious for nothing, but through prayer and supplication and with thanksgiving, to let my request be made known to God, and the peace of God that surpasses all understanding will guard my heart and mind through Christ Jesus. I will be okay! You tried to throw a couple of roadblocks at me in a desperate attempt to make my faith fail, but I rebuke you, in the name of Jesus! You cannot and will not have your way with me! I belong to Christ and have the victory over you, all your tricks, and all your deception! NOW, GET OUT OF HERE!"

The Word of God is a powerful weapon to use against the enemy. Using it will help you defeat the enemy and KEEP YOUR FOCUS. The battle is already won, and the victory is yours!

If you are reading this, it is a new day! What will you do with it?

Based on today's reading, what is God speaking to you?

____

____

____

____

____

____

____

____

____

____

____

____

____

____

Today's Scripture
Philippians 4:13 (KJV)
"I can do all things through Him who strengthens me."

Today, there is a new purpose, new opportunity, and new chance for you! Will you accept the newness of today? Whatever bothered you yesterday…whatever hurt you yesterday…whatever disappointed you yesterday…let it go! Walk in the "new" blessing of this day!

DAY 1

Enjoy Your Life

At times, I find myself focusing on the negative things in life. For example, if I have an ache or pain, do not feel well, or get upset about something—whether big or small—I tend to dwell on those things. I allow something that may be nothing to manifest into something detrimental in my mind.

The mind is immensely powerful. I believe we often underestimate the influence it has over our lives. The million-dollar question is: How do we control something so powerful?

Answer: Do not allow just anything into our minds, and continuously feed it positivity.

What does that look like? Well, for me, I read my Bible, listen to inspirational music, have a heart of gratitude, and do those things that bring me joy, happiness, and peace. It may look different for you, but the idea is to permit ONLY GOOD VIBES into your space…your mind. Though the day may bring disappointment and discouragement at times, remember it is still a new day. Make every effort to make the best of each day, regardless of its circumstances.

There are days when I want to press a do-over button, but the truth is that an attitude adjustment and perspective change can make all the difference in my perception of that day.

My prayer for us all is that God will hold our hands, wipe our tears, and guard our hearts and minds those days when we are afraid, unsure, and insecure. I pray that through each day's surprises, we all do our part to KEEP our FOCUS on GOD and enjoy the gift of life every day.

If you are reading this, it is a new day! What will you do with it?

Based on today's reading, what is God speaking to you?

____

____

____

____

____

____

____

____

____

____

____

____

____

Today's Scripture
Philippians 4:8-9 (KJV)

"Finally, brothers, whatever is true, whatever is honorable, whatever is just, whatever is pure, whatever is lovely, whatever is commendable, if there is any excellence, if there is anything worthy of praise, think about these things. What you have learned and received and heard and seen in me—practice these things, and the God of peace will be with you."

Today, there is a new purpose, new opportunity, and new chance for you! Will you accept the newness of today? Whatever bothered you yesterday…whatever hurt you yesterday…whatever disappointed you yesterday…let it go! Walk in the "new" blessing of this day!